T0129740

SEE
OF THE
SPIRIT
NOT
OF THE
FLESH

ARI L. CHRISTIAN

WESTBOW
P R E S S®
A DIVISION OF THOMAS NELSON
& ZONDERVAN

WestBow Press books may be ordered through booksellers or by contacting:

WestBow Press
A Division of Thomas Nelson & Zondervan
1663 Liberty Drive
Bloomington, IN 47403
www.westbowpress.com
1 (866) 928-1240

ISBN: 978-1-9736-4389-0 (sc)
ISBN: 978-1-9736-4390-6 (hc)
ISBN: 978-1-9736-4388-3 (e)

Library of Congress Control Number: 2018912906

Print information available on the last page.

WestBow Press rev. date: 12/10/2018

ACKNOWLEDGMENT

All credit goes to my Lord and Savior Jesus Christ.

I pray the Holy Spirit will move inside of you as
you read this book and help you to learn what your
needing from this subject. I pray that you will have
a spiritual revelation like I did so you can see things
with a new mind. Please read this prayer and pray
it, if you mean it, before reading this book.

"Dear Heavenly Father, I ask that you teach me as I begin
to study on how to see of the Spirit. I pray that you open
my mind and teach me what I need to learn. Holy spirit
guide me and bless me with knowledge and wisdom to
understand this book so that I can learn whatever it is I
need to learn in this moment. I thank you for teaching me
and always guiding me, In your Holy name I pray, Amen"

TABLE OF CONTENTS

Introduction 1

The Gospel 9

The Spirit versus the Flesh 15

My Testimony Of the Spirit and Of the Flesh 21

Ignorance isn't Bliss, Put on the Armor of God 43

Spiritual or Fleshly Attack 51

What Will You Do? 65

Challenge 69

Reflect 83

Decipher your past, Spiritually, So you can grow
Spiritually for a better future 85

INTRODUCTION

Have you ever heard a pastor in church tell you to live by the spirit and not the flesh? It sounds good, it sounds like it matches the word of God sense **Romans 8:13** tells us, *"For if you live according to the flesh you will die; but if by the Spirit you put to death the deeds of the body, you will live."* But is living by the spirit a literal thing? Is it a realistic thing we can do in our daily lives or does it just sound good to hear?

We are to live by the word of God, we are to follow what the bible tells us, we are to live according to God's word. So, if the bible tells us how to live, according to the Spirit, then it is a realistic and real thing no matter how crazy it sounds. We are to abide by the law but not live by the law, we need to first live by His grace. **Galatians 5:16-18** says, *"I say then: Walk in the Spirit, and you shall not fulfill the lust of the flesh. For the flesh lusts against the Spirit, and the Spirit against the flesh; and these are contrary to one another, so that you do not do the things that you wish. But if you are by the Spirit, you are not under the law."* If we choose to live and see of the Spirit, we will be living according to His grace. Following the ten commandments is great, but living by the Spirit does not mean walking on pins and needles afraid of breaking a law. It means allowing the Holy Spirit to guide you, to replace your wants and desires with what He wants for you, which in turn will give you the wants and the desires to live by His will and commandments without even trying, if you just let the Holy Spirit guide you.

Living and seeing of the Spirit means to see things as they are spiritually, to educate us on the spiritual realm around us that even though we cant see it, it is indeed there. **Psalms 91:11-12** says, *"For He shall give His angels charge over you, To keep you in all your ways. In their hands they shall bear you up, Lest you dash your foot against a stone."* Even though we don't physically see the angels doesn't mean they aren't there, it just means there is a spiritual realm around us that we cant see. Seeing of the spirit isn't just a good idea, its a real thing that we are supposed to make the reality of our lives so we can defend ourselves from the attacks of the devil and we can live with a sound mind. **2 Timothy 1:7** tells us, *"For God has not give us a spirit of fear, but of power and of love and of a sound mind."* Anything that tries to take away our sound mind is an attack, and if we can see it spiritually we can defend ourselves in Jesus' name to keep our sound mind that God wants us to have. Also, notice that it is mentioned that fear is a spirit, which will also show you that if you are in fear its because a spirit is literally attacking you to put you in fear.

My whole life I had struggled with stress and worrying, I allowed myself to think it was normal and that it happens to everyone, and it just meant that I really cared about whatever it is I was stressing or worrying about. But all I was doing was choosing to believe the lie satan wanted me to believe without even realizing it. God doesn't want us to stress, He tells us multiple times in the bible not to worry, and it is written 365 times in the bible not to fear. This means every day of the year, every year, we are not to fear. Stress and worry tend to stem from fear, if we eliminate fear, it makes it a lot easier to rid stress and worry. God has given us His word to stand on to eliminate these things and all attacks from our lives, but we have to be able to see the attack to defend ourselves from it, we have to be spiritually prepared and knowledgeable.

Im not saying I don't stress or worry anymore, the devil will always attack everyone, but now I know how to see things spiritually and how to tell when I am under attack, I can stand on Gods promises and stand on the word of God and Jesus Christ will save me from it, He will defend me from it rather then me dwelling on it for days on end, He has already beat this at the cross. The bible tells us we will face trouble, but if we learn to see of the Spirit, we can rely on the Holy spirit to deliver us from the troubles, and having a sound mind in the process.

If you have a child, and your child told you that they were upset over an issue, you would do everything in your power to make them happy because you love them. God loves us more than we could ever love our own children, thats really hard to fathom but it is true. And the bible tells us that He is the most High and has power over everything, so if we out of love would do anything to make our children happy, imagine what He wants to do for you to make you happy and in your sound mind, but you have to allow Him to do so. The Holy Spirit is gentle and will not force anything on you, you need to see spiritually so you can realize just how badly you need the Holy Spirit and how easy it is to hand things over to Him so you can live with the fruitfulness that God wants you to have.

I feel God wants me to write this book to show you the important revelation that I have recently encountered, so that you can stand tall and mighty in Him and live the life that He wants you to truly have, which I guarantee you is better than anything you could come up with on your own doing. *"For I know the thoughts that I think toward you, says the Lord, thoughts of peace and not of evil, to give you a future and a hope,"* **Jeremiah 29:11**. If your reading this, I'm guessing you felt led to it, and if thats the case, its probably time you learned how to really see and live of the Spirit and put away those fleshy desires that only bring you closer to the devils snare.

For any of this to make sense to you or really impact your life, its important that you know the true, unwatered down version of the gospel. If you have any hesitation on this subject at all, please go to the back of the book and read the chapter, "The Gospel". If you are unsure if you are saved, or if you don't know if you were baptized the way the bible instructs to, if there is any doubt or uncertainty at all please read it thoroughly so you can find out for sure if you are saved. We don't ever want to question our salvation, I was under the impression I was saved for a few years till God sent someone to me to point out that my baptism was inaccurate and I wasn't saved and was essentially an open target for the devil, don't let this be you. I was never taught to repent, to turn away from the sin I was still doing, I wasn't baptized in the Holy Spirit I was just symbolically dunked under water and that was it. I hear many people question if they need to be baptized of the water, or if the "sinners prayer" is good enough. My response is to turn to what Jesus said in **Joshua 3: 5**, *"Jesus answered, 'Most assuredly, I say to you, unless one is born of the water and the Spirit, he cannot enter the kingdom of God. That which is born of the flesh is flesh, and that which is born of the Spirit is spirit. Do not marvel that I said to you, 'You must be born again.'."* Notice, he doesn't say 'the sinners prayer is ok', or 'that it doesn't matter as long as you believe'. He said that you must be born of water and of the Spirit. To me, if thats not what He meant, I would think He wouldn't have said it, but if thats what He said, (and it is) who are we to argue? Are you willing to bet your salvation on "the sinners prayer" and just believing? Your salvation is on the line, make it simple, Jesus already made it simple for you by literally telling you what to do, doesn't get easier than that!

Ezekiel 36:25-27 says, *"Then I will sprinkle clean water on you, and you shall be clean; I will cleanse you from all your filthiness and from all your idols. I will give you a new heart and put a new spirit within you; I will take the heart of stone out of your flesh and give you a heart of flesh. I will put My Spirit within you and cause you to walk in My statutes, and you will keep My judgements and do them."* By being baptized of the Spirit and of the water, we are then able to receive a renewing of the mind, when we are water baptized we are dying with Christ and rising with Christ. Without that renewing of the mind we revert back to our old, sinful ways and we don't grow in the Spirit. For this book to make any sense to you and for you to truly understand how to see of the spirit and step away from operating in the flesh, you have to have the Holy Spirit within you to teach you how to achieve this fruitful reward. The bible promises His followers salvation, freedom, health, fruits of the Spirit and so much more, but if someone hasn't been truly saved, whether they agree with what the bible says or not, it doesn't apply to them, not yet anyways. If you are in any doubt at all, pay close attention to the next chapter, "The Gospel" and pray for God to show you what you need to do to ensure your salvation.

Or, if you are needing to understand a way to share

the gospel with loved ones, I still encourage you to read it. I have heard the gospel many times, but when it was explained to me this way, which is straight from the bible, it was as if a light bulb went on and it just made perfect sense. Hearing the gospel shared this way is what led to me getting saved.

THE GOSPEL

Its important that you know the true gospel, or none of this book will makes sense to you. Over the years, the gospel has gotten watered down and now days, sadly, people think they are christians as long as they believed some man died on a cross, but thats not the case, even atheist will admit a carpenter named Jesus died on a cross. Without the gospel and the truth of Jesus Christ, can you really call yourself a christian? A christian means to be like Christ, but if you don't know the gospel and you don't know His word, how can you say that you know Christ? So, incase you are unsure, lets do a crash coarse on the gospel, the unwatered down version.

In the beginning man walked with God. Adam and Eve were able to walk with God and life was good, there was no such thing as diseases or depression or anything bad, everything was good. Could you imagine a world with absolutely no evil at all? Think on this for a bit, meditate on it to see what man had before they gave it up. A world with no terrorist attacks, no shootings, no hate, no racism, no diseases, no sickness, no depression, no murderers, no rapists, no worry, no stress, no hate, nothing but love, peace and joy. This is what Adam and Eve had, a perfect world.

God showed them two trees, the tree of life and the one tree you can not eat form, the tree of knowledge of good and evil. God wanted them to live in bliss and peace and have the tree of life and be with Him, and to keep this all they had to do was stay away of the tree of knowledge of good and evil.

You might ask, why wouldn't God just keep the tree far away form them and not tell them about it if it was bad for them? The reason is because God wanted to know that they loved Him, that they cared about Him enough to follow His one and only rule for them. I know my spouse loves me because He chose to marry me on his own free will, no one was standing there forcing him to marry me. If he was forced, though he may treat me well, I would always be wondering if he really loved me, or if he said he loved me because he was forced too. His free will to marry me is how I know he truly loves me. This is why God will always give His people free will, because He doesn't want us to be forced in a relationship with Him, He wants to know we love Him and thats why we follow Him and have a relationship with Him.

So by asking them to follow His one rule, it was His was of knowing if they truly loved Him and wanted to be in a relationship with Him or not. Sadly, Adam and Eve fell for the devils tricks and ate from the tree of knowledge of good and evil, and this brought sin into the world. This single act brought sin into the world and it changed man, man was no longer able to receive God anymore because man was now unrighteous and sinful. God had to take away the tree of life and wasn't able to have a relationship with man anymore, this saddened God. He didn't want us to live a life with sin, sickness, disease and sadness. He didn't want us to be damned to Hell, so he found a solution to give us one last chance.

God sent Jesus, His one and only son down to die for us, so we can be saved and so through Jesus Christ we can have a relationship with God again, we can have the tree of life, we can be forgiven of our sins and we get saved from eternal damnation in hell, if we choose to follow Jesus. If we accept Jesus Christ as our Lord and savior and get water baptized we can have Jesus living within us, through the Holy Spirit. Jesus was pierced for our transgressions, He was crushed for our iniquities; the punishment that brought us peace was on Him, and by His stripes we are healed, **Isaiah 53:5**. Because God sent His one and only son to be beaten and pierced and then crucified so that we can have another chance to live a life in peace, with God, free from sickness and sin and in true joy with Jesus Christ as our Lord and Savior. God didn't have to do this, but because He loves us He did, now its our turn, will we choose Him back?

The gospel has to truly sink in and you have to truly believe it for you to understand what you are choosing when you choose to follow God, but once you believe it and you want to make Jesus Christ your Lord and Savior then you repent. You not only confess your sins, but you choose to not do them again, you pray for God to take the desire to keep doing these sins from you so that you will be free of them, this is the act of repentance. You cant just apologize for doing them, but you need to actually want to turn away from that sin. After you repent, you get baptized in the Holy Spirit and you get water baptized so you can have a renewing of the mind, you die in Christ and rise in Christ so you can be cleansed and made a new man/woman of God and you can be filled with the Holy Spirit, pray in tongues, heal the sick, cast out demons and you can finally live of the Spirit and not of the flesh.

If you need to be baptized, please pray first and ask God to show you a person who is truly filled with the Holy Spirit that can baptize you according to His word.

THE SPIRIT VERSUS THE FLESH

What exactly does it mean to see of the Spirit? Instead of seeing things as they are, with fleshly eyes, we need to try to see them for what they are spiritually. For example, lets say I am worrying over finances and it is really starting to stress me out so much that I am getting anxiety. To the "normal" eye, someone would say it the way they see it of the flesh, I am just anxious over finances. But if we see it for what it was spiritually, we can tell it is an attack from the devil himself. How do we tell this? We compare our issues straight to the word of God. Jesus specifically tells us, *"Therefor do not worry about tomorrow, for tomorrow will worry about its own things. Sufficient for the day is its own trouble,"* **Mathew 6:34**. Or if we go a few verses before to **Mathew 6:26**, *"Look at the birds of the air, for they neither sow nor reap nor gather into barns; yet your heavenly Father feeds them. Are you not of more value than they?"* First, Jesus tells us that if He takes care of the birds, why wouldn't He take care of you as well, because you are more valuable than birds. Then He continues by telling you not to worry about tomorrow. So if someone is stressing over finances, is it safe to say they are worrying about finances? Yes. And Jesus tells us not to worry, because just like He takes cares of the birds in the sky, He will also take care of you as well. And if we are stressing or worrying do we have a sound mind that God has given us? *"For God has not given us a spirit of fear, but of power and of love and of a sound mind,"* **2 Timothy 1:7**. So if our sound mind is gone, we are literally going against what Jesus has commanded us by worrying, then we can tell that we are under spiritual attack, because everything we are doing by the act of stressing and worrying is going against the word of God.

The first step is to see the problem, and recognize it so we can go to Jesus to save us from it. If we don't know we are under attack though, how can we ask to be saved from it? This is why we need to see things spiritually and not of the flesh. The world we live in sees things of the flesh, they don't see of the spirit. The bible tells us what is to be of the flesh versus of the Spirit in **Galatians 5 19-26**. *"Now the works of the flesh are evident, which are: adultery, fornication, uncleanness, lewdness, idolatry, sorcery, hatred, contentions, jealousies, outbursts of wrath, selfish ambitions, dissensions, heresies, envy, murders, drunkenness, revelries, and the like; of which I tell you beforehand, just as I also told you in the past, that those who practices such things will not inherit the kingdom of God. But the fruit of the Spirit is love, joy, peace, longsuffering, kindness, goodness, faithfulness, gentleness, self-control. Against such there is no law. And those who are Christ's have crucified the flesh with its passions and desires. If we live in the Spirit, let us also walk in the Spirit. Let us not* *become conceited, provoking one another, envying one another."* To see things of the flesh and Spirit can be as simple as starting with something I like to call the rubber band challenge, although its not really challenging its quite simple. Wear a rubber band on your wrist and anytime you start doing anything in the list of fleshy acts above, snap the wrist band to bring awareness that you are literally doing a fleshly act the bible tells us not to do if we want to inherit the kingdom of God. Next, anytime you start to do anything that goes against the word of God (ie stress, worry, fear) snap the rubber band and realize what you are doing is an attack. Later I will explain what to do when under attack, but first we really need to understand when we are under attack. If you feel any negative emotion whatsoever, snap the band so you can become aware of when something is coming against your sound mind and peace that God wants you to have.

If something negative is going on in your life that you literally have control over (the way you act or what you are thinking or saying or doing) re-evaluate and think, could this be an attack? If we allow negative thoughts to take root, that is an attack because it goes against our sound mind. If we are living in fear/stress/worry/anxiety we are under attack. If you keep saying rude things to people without even meaning too, or if you are meaning too, you are under attack. God doesn't want us to be mean to others, as Christians we need to be like Christ, was Jesus mean to people? No. **Mathew 12:33-37** Jesus says, *"Either make the tree good and its fruit good, or else make the tree bad and its fruit bad; for a tree is known by its fruit. Brood of vipers! How can you, being evil, speak good things? For out of the abundance of the heart the mouth speaks. A good man out of the good treasure of his hear brings forth good things, and an evil man out of the evil treasure brings for evil things. But I say to you that for every idle word men may speak, they will give account of it in the day of judgment. For by your words you will be justified, and by your words you will be condemned."* This tells us, that by saying something mean to someone you are literally going against what Jesus told us not to do, and this is an attack that you are feeding into. **Proverbs 18:21** says, *"Death and life are in the power of the tongue, and those who love it will eat its fruit."* What you say matters, don't give life to dangerous words.

If you randomly feel like you should sleep with someone other than your spouse, you are under attack. ANYTHING that goes against the word of God is an attack. This is why it is crucial that we all know the word of God. You cant see of the Spirit if you dont know the word of God, you will get confused and lost. You have to educated yourself by asking the Holy Spirit to teach you as you read your bible day and night. **Joshua 1:8** tells us, *"This Book of the Law* *shall not depart from your mouth, but you shall meditate in it day and night, that you may observe to do according to all that is written in it. For then you will make your way prosperous, and then you will have good success."* Picture each book in the bible as a personal letter, to you, to show you right from wrong, to educate you, to show you how to protect yourself and inherit the kingdom of God. Picture the bible as a letter to you from God to show you the truth of life.

MY TESTIMONY OF
THE SPIRIT AND
OF THE FLESH

Im going to share my testimony to show you examples of how things happen of the spirit, but how we perceive it in the flesh. Let me start by explaining that I am not using real names in this book because most of the people in my testimony have not found Jesus yet, they are still living of the flesh and they dont know the truth, they dont know Jesus and I dont want their reputations to get shattered because they are lost, and I dont want this book to push them farther away from God which is what I feel would happen if I used their names. I feel it would make them resent God, and because I only want good to come from this I have made it anonymous for my families sake.

I grew up in southern California till I was about 6 with my mom and siblings. My mother has had a tougher upbringing than mine and unfortunately has never found her way out of it. She grew up with a dad who had a dark sense of humor and was interested in satanic things without even knowing it. You see, her father was a lost man, he was into the new things that others were into in the 70's and that involved tarot cards and possibly sorcery, which mentioned earlier in **Galations 5 19-26**, lets us know is of the flesh and not something we should do . He once had picture of the devil in his living room till my grandmother made him get rid of it. But he was mean and abusive so she let him have a room to keep all those things in the house as long as the kids didn't see it. She didn't understand the spiritual harm she was allowing into her home. By allowing sorcery related items in your home you are going against the word of God by entertaining things of the flesh, and you are allowing spirits in your home that will bring harm and chaos. This is probably why my grandfather was abusive and cheated on my grandmother, and was a pedophile. He was spiritually following the devil, whether he believed it or not, he made allegiance to him the day he brought those items and a picture of the devil into his home, and acted on taking advantage of the innocent.

When one bad spirit comes around and you entertain it, its like a flood gate, more will come. The spirit of addiction came right after the spirit of anger, perversion and hate and it took root in my mother. She started using drugs when she was fourteen and is still currently using to this day. The spirits that she unknowingly entertains are the reason she is depressed, sad, high all the time and filled with fear and guilt and confusion.

She didn't know how to be a good parent with all these spiritual attacks going on, in and around her, she couldn't be. But by her participating in fleshly desires like getting high and entertaining hobbies that most people on drugs entertain, she brought in my siblings and me into her mess. The company she kept were people who were just as spiritually lost as she was, the bible tells us iron sharpens iron, you are what you surround yourself with, **Proverbs 27:17**, *"As iron sharpens iron, So a man sharpens the countenance of his friend."* . If you want to be with druggies, you will be a druggie, if you want to hang out with Spirit filled Christians, you will be a Spirit filled Christian. My mother was lost and didn't know any better, and the short years she did have custody of me, I was molested twice before I turned four. My mother didn't know how to live of the Spirit and turn from her fleshly ways because she didn't know Jesus, and because of that, all of her kids were open targets to the devil. **John 10:10**, *"The thief does not come except to steal, and to kill and to destroy. I have come that they may have life, and that they may have it more abundantly."* The devil can only do this to people who are not saved, why? Because if you are saved you have the Holy Spirit inside of you, Jesus has already defeated the devil and has given you the authority to do so as well. But without Jesus, all havoc breaks loose. Because my mother didn't have Jesus in her life, she was mean, high and abusive to me and my siblings and she has never felt true peace and happiness. Because my mother didn't know Jesus, my sister didn't know Jesus and didn't know true love and searched for it in all the wrong places and still does today. Because we didn't have Jesus in our lives, my brother got caught up in the wrong crowd and was murdered in his early twenties.

My dad got custody of me when I was six and things

did get better, I wasn't beat anymore and I was in a better environment without anyone on drugs. I was put in a well known daycare before and after school sense my dad worked late, but what no one knew was that the lady who ran the daycare was married to a man who was into pedophilia, so I joined as many after school activities as I could so I wouldn't have to go there anymore. I was thankful to play sports in school for this reason. So I played sports all year round so while my dad was at work I had somewhere safe to go. The spirit of shame came on me quick as well, which is why I couldn't tell my dad about any of these things, I couldn't tell anyone because I felt like it was my fault for attracting this kind of behavior, thats what the devil wanted me to think. I actually kept it inside till I married my husband, he was the first person I was able to really share this stuff with, and it was because I knew he was a man of God and would see it for what it was, spiritual attacks from the devil and I knew he was a safe person to tell without any form of judgement. But as a child I held it in and kept to my self a lot because of it. You see, spirits work together, when one gets a foothold it attracts many other familiar spirits because they see you as an easy, already established target.

Have you ever had the sudden urge to just go to the bar and let off some steam by tossing a few back? This is another spiritual attack, because once you are under the influence, you are not righteous in God and the Holy Spirit cant protect you, you are now open and your now fair game for the devil because the bible is clear when it comes to not being a drunkard **Ephesians 5:18**, *"And do not be drunk with wine, in which is dissipation; but be filled with the Spirit,"*. This lets us know that you can not be filled with the Spirit and be drunk, because being drunk allows the wrong kind of spirits to entertain you and when that happens, because of the sin you are at that moment entertaining, the Holy Spirit wont protect you. When we walk in sin we are not walking with God, we have to turn from sin to walk with God and be protected by Him. God doesn't tell us not to get drunk to try to take the fun away, He warns us not to get drunk so we can stay filled with the Spirit, His Spirit, to protect us. He has an amazing reason for everything he commands, its always for our best interest. But when we go against the word of God we are not protected, which is why we need to know His word, so we stay protected.

When you are drunk you tend to say and do things that you would never normally say or do, this is because spirits are now operating inside of you. For example, the spirit of anger might cause you to get in a bar fight even though your normal dimeanor is to be a nice person. The spirit of adultery might cause you to sleep with someone and cheat on your spouse even though when sober you would never do that. The spirit of jealousy might make you freak out on your spouse for flirting with someone when they really weren't, the spirit of jealousy was lying to you but now you are in a fight with your spouse. These are reasons why God tells us not to be a drunkard, its for our own spiritual safety that then turns into fleshy acts.

My father didn't know Jesus either, one day he got wasted and slept with a women he wasn't in a relationship with and it took that one time for them to have my little sister. The next ten years they would break up, get back together, break up and get back together like a viscous cycle. They weren't in love with each other, they tried to make the best of it and my dad turned back to the spirit of addiction but this time with alcohol. This caused a lot of fights and not a lot of parental supervision in my teen years, so basically I had free range to do as I wanted. And for a teenager who doesn't know Jesus, has self esteem issues from being molested, and a lot of built up anger and frustration from her home "family" life, this can be dangerous. I started partying hard and sense the spirit of addiction was already in my family I was an easy target and started doing drugs in high school which led to me dropping out and getting my ged.

I had experienced lies upon lies from the devil; my mother didn't love me because she chose drugs over me, my father was miserable so he drank, I was pathetic because I didn't have a mother (this was said by many false christians at fake churches, believe it or not), I was gross because I was molested as a kid, I was gross because the babysitters husband touched me, I was worthless. These lies played in my head because my family didn't know Jesus, and getting high felt good because I didn't feel any of that and I was accepted by the people getting high with me. This was what the devil wanted, he wanted me to live by the flesh; get high, have low self esteem and feel worthless. So I went down the rabbit hole, I did lots of drugs and dated many guys, one guy in particular that was way too old for me because it made me feel wanted and not rejected. The devil will get in your head and make you feel less than so you will lower your standards and waste your time doing things you shouldn't do and being with people you shouldn't be with because it keeps you further away from God. If you dont see things in the spiritual, you would never think it was the devil causing all this strife you would classify it as a fleshy and worldly thing like "addiction is a genetics thing and thats why I was going through these things" and "although its not normal it happens".

The devil wanted to bring me down and make me feel rejected, my whole life. When I was using drugs I started to hang out with a cousin of mine, he was a good ten years older then me, I had just turned eighteen and he had been off and on drugs for a while now. The devil knew this and wanted to bring him back down, so it was no coincidence that I randomly hung out with him one day when I other wise never had hung out with him before, I loved my cousin but the age gap was pretty big and we never had anything in common because of that. My cousin and I hung out one "random" day and he told me his wife cheated on him and he was getting a divorce and was currently clean but wanted to use, and sense I was there and high he asked me for some drugs. I told him I didn't have any, which was the truth, I didn't even know a drug dealer, I was that new to the game. Within five minutes he called his dealers and had drugs ready for pick up and because I was the one with him when he chose to use again, his immediate family blamed me for everything. It didn't matter that he was already wanting to use to numb the pain of his divorce, or he was way older then me and more of an influence on me then I was on him, and that he was the one who called the hook up, it was still my fault in their eyes.

This is what the devil wanted, the devil knew if I was the one with him when he used some of my family would hate me and reject me and it would work to his plan of making me feel worthless. No one in my family knew Jesus, no one thought or saw of the spirit, everyone had deep routed spirits of anger and loved nothing more than to single people out because it took the attention away from their alcohol and drug addiction problems. Addiction is a spiritual attack, people will see it and see it of the flesh and call it a genetic trait passed down, but if multiple generations have this problem, its a generation curse the devil has placed on your family, its all spiritual.

During this time a different family member committed suiced, he was depressed and couldn't fight it anymore and everyone around him was so lost in their own spiritual battles of addiction and depression that they didn't realize how bad he was struggling. He was only thirty and he couldn't fight the fight on his own and he took his life. None of us can fight the fight on our own, which is why we need Jesus. His parents and siblings were obviously upset and felt an extreme sense of guilt because they felt as though they should have noticed he was that bad, but thats because the devil wanted them to feel guilty, so they would lean in closer to the spirits of anger and addiction. So they tried to point the finger of blame on anyone who they thought was a bad influence and I was one of the unfortunate targets. At the funeral reception his sibling asked me to leave, not in the nicest words, which by this point I had been clean for a while now and wasn't even using anymore, I was even signed up for the military and was doing great. But she didn't care, because I used to do drugs and her brother knew that somehow it was my fault and I couldn't be there. It didn't matter that I was never around her brother to be a bad influence on, her brother was fifteen years older than me, she was using too and was now a drunk even though I had been clean for a few months before this happened, there was no reasoning with her she hated me.

The devil wanted me to feel rejection and when you feel it from your family thats a big hit. I was in a new relationship, with someone who was clean and he happened to be friends with my family, yet when it came to family bbq's he was invited and asked not to bring me, another sign of rejection. His family didn't like me because I was white and not a catholic, to his hispanic family that was a big deal so I was rejected by them as well. But no matter how hard the devil was trying to bring me back to the drugs it didn't work, because God took the urge away from me. The last night I ever used, I was sitting outside by myself looking up at the stars and I just felt peace, for the first time, (which is something you never feel after getting high) and I felt like I didn't need to do this anymore, I heard a voice in my head say I didn't need this and it was time to quit. It didn't make sense but the urge to use drugs left instantly and has never come back. I had tried to quit before and failed, but after this night it was easy and effortless. Ten years later and I am still going strong and haven't used meth because Jesus took that addiction for me at the cross. **John 6:44**, *"No one can come to Me unless the Father who sent Me draw* *him; and I will raise him up at the last day."* This marked the beginning of changes for me that would after a couple years due to my stubbornness and ignorance, lead me to get saved. Everyone I did drugs with back then is either dead today, in jail or on the verge of death. God had bigger plans for me and He knows our hearts, He knows if we are willing to turn to Him before we ever do or not.

I got pregnant when I was 20 and it was a surprise, my boyfriend and I had just broke up and I had moved out into a house with my friend. I was terrified. I was working full time as a receptionist, I was never able to join the military because I had scoliosis, so I was going back to school and working in the clerical field full time. I had been clean for a year and a half and was doing great, minus the break up, and when I found out I was pregnant that made a huge impact. The dad wanted me to get an abortion and offered me two grand to abort the baby, I wasn't religious but I just morally couldn't do it. He didn't like that so every morning as I would wake up with morning sickness, he would send me a text saying how much he hated me, how I would be a horrible mom and how he was going to take the baby from me so I could never see it. Every morning he would text me this kind of stuff, and then he got his friends in it and they began texting me every morning saying how the baby would be better off dead and I dont deserve to be a mom and a I am the worst person ever just doing this to get back together with my ex. They were all crazy but the harassing made me feel sicker than I had already felt. This was the devil once again trying to make me feel rejected and horrible, he wanted me to get an abortion and he thought this would work. But when I rose above it and didn't, a car accident happened on my way home from work and I was involved in it, I was hit by a drunk driver. I went to the er and they said it was unclear if it was from the accident or the stress but either way I lost the baby.

I know now that it was the devil, he comes to steel, kill and destroy. But back then I didn't know that, I was confused and lost and in pain. The doctor gave me a bunch of pain medication and that brought on a narcotics addiction. For the next six months there wasn't a moment of the day that I wasn't emotionally numb from the pills. My ex took the news obviously well and then wanted to get back together sense their was no baby in the picture anymore, it made me sick. When I told him no, he stalked me for a few months. The devil was doing works on him as well that I didn't understand it back then but today makes perfect sense the spiritual battle he has going on in him and his family.

My roommates didn't use drugs or anything like that just drank on the weekends and worked good jobs, and it made me feel bad because I wanted to sink low in my own whole and didn't want judgment for it. So I moved out and got my own place where I was able to let my freak flag fly. I started to hang out with people that I didn't need to be around and fell so low I even stripped for three months to pay rent. I made anywhere from ninety to a thousand dollars per hour, and only had to work 4 hours a week so it was easy to maintain with my pill addiction. I had a bodyguard drive me so I didn't have to drive while using pills and even started dating the guy, and eventually married him. The devil wanted to tie me down with a guy that would not bring me closer to God but pull me further away. He was placing people in my life to keep me down and this was another way.

We had moved out of California to get away from the drama and believe it or not I got a job as a preschool teacher in a church. I obviously left out on my resume a bit when it came to most recent jobs. But this job and this church helped me, I started to seek God and I really did love my job. The devil didn't like this, he tried to put bad people in our lives to keep me down, he had my then husband invite his coworker and his wife over for dinner. As we sat there, the guys wife declared that she was a white witch, but said it was ok because she was a christian and believed in God too.. I didn't know what she was talking about but it gave me the chills so I politely tried to change the subject, and later I said they couldn't come over anymore. It took me a long time to realize that was literally the devil trying to bring people over to pull me closer to him. Now I have learned, there really are witches out there today, and their is no such thing as a good one. Sure, she believed in God, but her God is the devil not the Lord Jesus Christ. Its all spiritual, when you start to seek or grow to God the devil will place people or things in your life, or even ideas to try to pull you away from God, its not a coincidence, he literally has nothing better to do and he is more than patient enough to keep trying to keep you down. He tried to place a person in my life who was living of the flesh by being involved in sorcery and was hoping that I would be intrigued and join in. Thankfully I steered clear of it, and today I know that because Galatians chapter 5 tells us about actions of the flesh, mentioning sorcery among them (refer to **Galations 5 19-26**) I know it was an attack to try to keep me involved with the wrong group to prevent me from seeking God.

I started to seek God and my then husband wanted nothing to do with it, we were already having troubles, I knew we were never in love and got married out of fear of not wanting to be alone. It only took a few months for things to start to get bad, I seeked God and he wanted nothing to do with God. He wouldn't go to church with me and we grew further apart because I was finding this new part in my life that felt great and he was falling deeper in his anger filled hole that he didn't want to let go of. Not even a year into our marriage we ended it, he went back to his alcoholic family where he wanted to be and I wanted to be far from, and I turned closer to God and got baptized.

However, I didn't know the church I got baptized in didn't believe in baptism as dying in Christ, and rising in Christ, or having a renewing of the mind, or casting out anything that needed to be casted out, or praying in tongues, and no repenting. They believed it was a symbolic thing only, why? Because that was the devils way of keeping them from baptizing people the way the bible tells you too, if you are not baptized according to the bible, then you aren't baptized, you just dunked your head under water, nothing more. The devil was hoping I would never get really baptized and that I would stay uneducated about this, because I didn't have the holy spirit in me yet, and he wanted it to stay that way.

Some time later I found the guy God wanted me to marry, and everything worked flawlessly. God had it all planned out, he found me a place to live three states away to be closer to him so we could date more before getting married, and he found me a place to live in the matter of a few hours. I had little money in my account but I didn't have stress or worry I felt like this was what I needed to do and that God was guiding it. When it came time for us to get a home, I didn't even try, God sent someone to me at the gym to offer us his home for sell and we got it for an incredibly, cheap price. It was worth way more then what we had to pay for it. Our wedding worked out great, everything we needed for the wedding happened to be on sale or almost free and we had the entire wedding planned and paid for in one week, it was amazing.

We got pregnant on our wedding night and the fear from my first miscarriage came flooding back in. We had another miscarriage. This was hard to accept, because it didn't make sense to me, I thought we were living by His will, I thought we were following God and protected by Him so I didn't get how another miscarriage could happen. I didn't know why God would do this or allow this, it about broke my heart. I stopped reading my bible for a while, I wasn't mad at God, I was just confused and wanted to shut my mind off. But I became obsessed with having a baby, I bought a bunch of ovulation tests and pregnancy tests and every month when I would start my period I would secretly break down and cry.

During this time, my cousin who I used to use drugs with, had past away, he overdosed. He had been clean for a while before I moved out of California, we actually became better friends when he was sober and it was amazing. But he had demons he couldn't shake off and after a year of being clean went back to using. I was so sad when I heard the news, and I knew going to the funeral wouldn't help because all the extended family who would be there hated my guts. So I sent some money to help with the services and asked his brother for the funeral time incase I was able to fly out and go. But, of coarse, he didn't respond or tell me, an old friend told me the day before and by then there was no way I could go. But I think it was for the best, I would have been viciously attacked by family members that are still drunks and drug users and it would have done more harm then good. But it was all spiritual, the overdose was the devil telling him reasons to get higher and higher to numb out the pain. His families hatred for me was the devil filling their hearts with hate and numbing their minds with drugs and alcohol.

The devil can plant a thought in your mind, a thought to make you feel like you should get drunk or high and makes the thought hard to ignore so you cave and do it. This is how it happens spiritually, it isn't normal to have these thoughts pop in your head, if you get them you need to realize it is the devil trying to get a foothold on you and you need Jesus to be able to cast it out. Anything that goes against the word of God is spiritual and are planted on you from the devil himself, and he will use your flesh to make the cravings or the attack hard to resist, thats his goal. If you cant separate flesh from spirit you will fail and fall into the devils snare over and over again, I know I did for years.

One day my husband was watching youtube videos about people praying on the streets in Jesus' name for healing and people were getting healed, in this particular video they had one leg shorter then the other that grew out to equal length in Jesus name. He was so excited about it but I was skeptical. I knew Jesus could heal but I said there was no way to tell if that was real or if people were faking the healing because they wanted youtube views. My husband prayed that I would open up to it and three days later I had a knock on my office door. I opened it and these people were just needing camping services for the night, I got them signed up and they asked if my back hurt. I said I had scoliosis and it always hurt. They asked if they could pray and I said sure, then they started praying in tongues which honestly weirded me out a bit, but I felt this warm and hot feeling go through my body. Then they prayed over my legs and one leg grew out a couple inches to match the other, I didn't even know one was shorter. They gave me a dvd on baptism and the Holy Spirit and my husband and I watched it immediately. I had LOTS of questions. Because I saw how they baptized people, according to the bible, and I realized I didn't have that at all. Before this at our new church that is spirit filled the pastor talked about the biblical way to baptize and what he said matched what this dvd said, and I had asked previously if we needed to redo our baptisms and my husband didn't think we needed too.

After watching this dvd though, he said we needed to

redo our baptisms, and I felt like we needed to as well. We called them and asked them if they could come talk to us and they did, we stayed up talking past midnight about the unwatered down gospel, the way we are to be baptized according to the bible. We even talked about my miscarriage and this is when I learned that the devil steels, kills and destroys, and that he took the babies away and he was able to because even though I thought I was living according to Gods will I really wasn't, I wasn't really baptized and I was still living in sin. I believed the lie the devil wanted me to believe so I wouldn't truly follow Gods will. I was getting drunk on the weekends, never had a proper baptism of the Holy Spirit, I didn't ever think what God wants or prayed for His guidance I just tried to follow the ten commandments and that was it. Because I wasn't following God or saved I was an open target and the devil wanted to try to find ways to get me to turn on God, and he thought taking my babies would make that happen.

That night we asked them to baptize us down at the spring the next morning, and they did. They weren't planning on staying in our little town that night, but God led them there, He used them to get us to see the truth to get saved. I stopped trying to get pregnant and I trusted in Gods plan for the first real time ever. I didn't care anymore if that meant having our own kids or adopting I knew Gods plan would be perfect.

When I got baptized I felt weightless and for the first time complete peace. We learned to pray in tongues and life hasn't been the same ever sense. Now I can truly rely on the Holy Spirit, when Im under attack God gives me the way out. A year later we had a beautiful baby girl which has opened my eyes even more to what Gods love is like. Everything around us is spiritual, the devil tries to keep us from reaching God, he had tried my whole life and still tries today, but when you can step back and see things spiritually, you can defend yourself and truly live the life that God wants you to have.

IGNORANCE ISN'T BLISS, PUT ON THE ARMOR OF GOD

I used to think that ignorance is bliss, and that as long as I didn't entertain evil things like demons or spirits than they wouldn't bother me and I would be safe to do as I please. But what I didn't know, was that was the lie the devil wanted me to believe, because he didn't want me to know the truth and be spiritually educated to defend myself. The truth is, there is a spiritual realm around us, wether we see it or not, it is there. I used to think that as long as I didn't entertain evil, I was protected. But the truth is, if you don't understand the evil around you, then you are defenseless and cant protect yourself. If you can see with your spiritual eyes, and not of the flesh, then you can identify the evil that is there and defend yourself by standing on the word of God, and His promises.

Once you get baptized in the Holy spirit and water baptized (you need to do both), then you have the Holy Spirit living inside of you. **Joshua 10:8** tells us, *"And the Lord said to Joshua, 'Do not fear them for I have delivered them into your hand; not a man of them shall stand before you.'."* With Jesus on your side and the Holy Spirit inside you, the devil cant defeat you. He will try, but you can over come it because Jesus is with you and he is the strongest of all. Its no longer you against evil, its God fighting in you against the evil, and with God you cant lose. But in order to know how to really give all to God and let Him lead the way and protect you, you need to know Him by knowing His word.

Once you start to seek God, the devil hates it because you are now learning how to protect yourself from the devils attacks. He will try to throw distractions at you to prevent you from having the time to follow through with your bible study. **Joshua 1:8** tells us to meditate on the word of God day and night, we need to do this and the devil will do whatever he can to try to get us to forget, or be distracted or too tired. That is an attack and you aren't even aware of it. Consider the bible like a play book to defeat your opponent. Football teams get to watch tapes of their opponents before they play them, to see how they operate and work. Imagine if you were a football coach and you gained access to the other teams playbook, you could then see what plays they run and you will have a winning edge to beat them. Thats how we should look at the bible, yes its a way to know God, but its also a way to learn about how we should be living spiritually and how to be protected, strong, filled with wisdom and knowledge so we are no longer victims to the devils schemes. The bible is our playbook to beat him.

God calls us to wear the Armor of God, **Ephesians 6:10-16**, *"Be strong in the Lord and in His mighty power. Put on the full armor of God so that you can take your stand against the devils schemes."* To do this, you must first put on the Helmet of Salvation by believing that Jesus died for our sins and rose again. Once you have been saved and you believe that Jesus died for our sins and rose again, then you have successfully applied the Helmet of Salvation.

We all need to use the Belt of Truth, we must compare our actions to the word of God. This keeps us from straying and giving into the worlds beliefs. Anyone can fall victim to this, I have even had a spirit filled pastor accidentally give me advice that literally went against the word of God. I know it wasn't his intent but if I wouldn't have gone home and matched what he said to the word of God, I would have gone against Gods word and it would have caused a lot of pain and strife in my life. Always always always match up your actions and your word to the word of God, its the only word that matters.

The Breast Plate of Righteousness tells us to be honest, good, humble and fair to others. We must never become filled with pride, we have to always remain humble, and whenever something great happens give credit to where its due, God, not you. You cant be humble and righteous if you are filled with pride. If you share the gospel with someone and they get saved, you didn't save them, Jesus did. If you get a raise at work or write a book or win an award, its not on your doing, its because of God. You cant walk with God if you walk in sin, being righteous requires us to be honest, humble, good and fair.

The Sword of the Spirit is the word of God and we must take it with us everywhere we go and use it, live it, and know it. Without the word of God, you don't really know God and you don't have the offensive weapon to defeat the devil, you become weak and an easy target. Imagine seeing it with your spiritual eyes, imagine you are under attack, a demon is literally whispering lies into your ears hoping that you will believe them and start to fear, worry or stress. But as you speak the word of God, a sword of light comes piercing out of your mouth and pushes that pesky demon away. Visualize this every time, you may have to repeat this as the devil is determined to attack you, we need to be determined to stand in our victory, from victory to victory, never from defeat to victory. Meditate on that, God keeps us from victory to victory, when you fall under attack, cast it out, speak the word of God and then worship God and see your light sword shoot out of your mouth and push the devil away as you praise God.

Next, we have to step into the Gospel of Peace by being right with God and being contended in troubled times. Jesus said peacemakers were blessed, it is our job to keep the peace. This doesn't mean let people walk all over you, but one main reason why people don't want to be christians today is because non believers see christians as hypocrites due to being judgmental. If you are being judgmental to someone, you are not keeping the peace you are stirring the drama pot. Christians are a representative of Christ, therefore we need to be the light in the darkness, not the other way around, we need to draw people to God not push them away, we need to keep the peace. I have many loved ones that I care deeply about who have a resentment that they don't even understand, all caused by fake christians who were judgmental and mean or who have made false statements claiming its the word of God when it wasn't even close to it. We are supposed to guide the lost to Jesus by showing His love, not keeping people away from Jesus by doing the devils work for him.

Lastly but certainly not least we need our Shields of Faith. We need to be sure that God will keep His promises, He will protect us when we are tempted to doubt. We need our faith in God to fight through the hard times when we are tempted. When you feel under attack and you feel nervous or anxious, do what Jesus did when He was in the desert for forty days and was being tempted. He didn't sit there and argue with the devil, no, he declared the word of God and told the devil, "It Is Written" meaning the word of God is written and its all we need to stand on, its the truth. The devil hates that. If you are suffering with an emotion that takes away your sound mind declare, **2 Timothy 1:7**, " It is written, The Lord does not give us a spirit of fear, but of power, love and a sound mind. Anything that is trying to come against that I bind you and your strongmen and

I send you back to wherever it is you came from In Jesus name, for it is written." You may have to say it ten times a day, the devil is persistent but he hates hearing the word of God, because that is our offensive weapon and he has no power when it comes to God. Just declare the word of God and believe in what you are declaring. If you see yourself struggling with doubt, bind up all mind binding spirits and their strongmen and cast them out, then find a bible verse to stand on in your particular situation and declare it. "It is writtten, as He is, so are we of this world."

SPIRITUAL OR FLESHLY ATTACK

The bible tells us in **Isaiah 61:3** that there is a spirit of heaviness, this spirit knows our weaknesses and leaches onto us to cause anxiety, depression or any emotion that makes you feel a heavy burden on your chest. This spirit of heaviness is a spiritual attack that can cause your flesh to feel physical ailment. Attacks begin in the spiritual realm and then work towards your flesh. I used to get really bad anxiety because I was living a life of chaos and felt like no matter what I did to avoid it, the drama was seeking me out. I would literally hyperventilate and gasp for breath when it would get really bad. What I didn't know was it started as a spiritual attack. The life choices I was making (partying, getting drunk or high, sleeping around) these choices were welcoming in chaos and drama and disaster. It was welcoming in all of these bad spirits to run a train on my life. And then the spirit of heaviness would come in and weigh me down making me want to escape the anxiousness by going and getting high again, which would just make things worse and make the cycle repeat itself. There is all forms of heaviness, it can be a heaviness due to stressing over finances, which is still spiritual because the bible tells us not to worry about tomorrow (finances included). Anything that causes you to feel anxious, stressed or worrisome is a form of heaviness and is a spiritual attack.

In **2 Timothy 1:7** the bible tells us that fear is a spirit, anything causing you to have fear is a spiritual attack. If something is happening that is taking away your sound mind and your peace, odds are it is a spiritual attack caused by spirits that the devil has sent your way. The devil watches your every move and has all the patience in the world to find out what will send you over or what will cause you to fall from God.

For example, I know of a couple who fears being broke, so much so that when they are with out work they seek God but the second they get work they forget all about God. God can put us in positions to get great jobs, but so can the devil. The devil watched this family and knew that they only searched for God when they had nothing, but once they were rolling in the big bucks they didn't care about God. They traded in the spirit of fear for the spirit of greed and now they do nothing but work to buy all of these expensive things to fill the void that they still have because they don't know Jesus. It doesn't matter what they buy though, the excitement fades then they are still left searching for anything to fill the void, yet they never turned back to God because they didn't want to make a commitment.

Another example is looking at the spirit of control and the spirit of adultery. This couple had a few kids and the mom stayed at home and took care of the kids while the dad worked. The dad was always at work so the rare times he was home, he had no idea what the kids liked or ate or anything so the wife felt the need to tell him what the kids liked and didn't like and what items went where. She felt like he had no idea so if she didn't tell him he would get the kids food they didn't like and it'd go to waste, or he would loose items by putting them away in the wrong spot, or he would do something the kids didn't like and make them cry. In her mind she was just trying to help her husband to understand. From her husbands point of view she was being controlling and nagging and making him feel worthless and like a stranger in his own home. See, the devil wanted them to feel distant rather then closer together, he wanted to tear them apart so he sent the spirit of control and nagging to his wife and the spirit of irritation and anger to the husband. In their minds, they were both justified but with God out of the picture all guidance left and the spirits took advantage.

The husband wanted to feel wanted and worthy but didn't know how to talk to his wife about it because he was so irritated. The wife was now angry because she could feel her husbands irritation and she could tell he was slipping away. Then the spirit of addiction comes in and puts the idea in his head to just go to the bar and have one drink to blow some steam off when you get off work before you go home, she will never know and you will feel better. So he acts off the idea and goes to the bar for just one beer, but soon the spirit comes back and tells him one more wont hurt, so he has one more. Before you know it he was drunk and all kinds of spirits are now operating in him, including the spirit of adultery. A lady at the bar makes him feel wanted which is what he has been seeking and he goes for it because he is drunk and the spirits lead him, now he has cheated on his wife and their family is split up. It literally can happen this fast.

You see, the devil sends his familiar spirits to spy on you and see what bait you will go for and what bait wont interest you at all. He knows your tactics and likes and dislikes, so why not learn this to defend yourself? If the married couple above knew how to see spiritually, they could have prayed for God to guide them, they could have seen the spirits operating trying to make them controlling and irritated and they could have cast them out before they were able to take root. **1 Corinthians 10:13** reminds us that God doesn't allow us to be tempted with more than we can bare, and he provides the way out, *"No temptation has overtaken you except such as is common to man; but God is faithful, who will not allow you to be tempted beyond what you are able, but with temptation will also make the way of escape, that you may be able to bear it."* If the spirit of fear is taunting us, God knows we can over come it through Jesus, all we have to do is keep declaring, "Spirit of fear I bind you and send you back to wherever it is you came from for it is written, the Lord does not give us a spirit of fear but of power, love and a sound mind." If you feel irritated then cast out the spirit of irritation, whatever emotion you are feeling cast it out in Jesus name because it is coming against your sound mind and that is going against the word of God, then declare the word of God out loud and praise Him, the devil hates being around when you praise Jesus.

Its sad but there are a lot of Sunday Christians out there, meaning they claim to know God, they read their bibles and pray and worship but only on Sundays, every other day of the weak they do as they please. These fake christians are the reasons why real Christians are called hypocrites. These fake Christians are the ones who fall under attack even more so because the devil says to himself, "They claim to be Christians so if I can make them suffer and make them look like drunks or give them a disease and they die people will blame God because He allowed that to happen to one of His followers." But the truth is, if you live in sin you are not a Christian and you are not protected by God because you are not living according to His will. The rest of the world doesn't know that though, and it makes christianity look bad so the devil loves to seek prey on fake christians. Remember, to be a christian means to be like Christ, if you only practice this one day a week then you're not being like Christ, Christ is not a one day a week God. He is all day every day, and to be like Him we must be 24/7 christians.

We must know the word of God to know what is an

attack and whats not, I cant stress this enough. When Jesus died on the cross he bore our inequities. **Isaiah 53:5** says, *"But he was wounded for our transgressions, He was bruised for our iniquities; The chastisement for our peace was upon Him, And by His stripes we are healed."* This bible verse has a lot of meat to it. Lets break it down and start with transgressions, which means an act of going against a law or rule, a synonym is sin. Jesus was pierced for our sins, so that we could repent and be forgiven and not be damned to hell. He was crushed for our iniquities, which means sin and evilness. So He was crushed for our sin and evil doing, of our unrighteousness so that we could repent and become righteous. This punishment is why we are able to live in peace, if we choose to surrender all and follow Jesus. By His wounds we are healed. If we look at what healed means, the definition states that it means to be cured, to recover, to be repaired and restored, to be sound and healthy. By His wounds we are healthy, made whole and new, we are no longer sick so any sickness that tries to come against the word of God and tries to take away what Jesus did for us is an attack and needs to be casted out. God is the almighty and has the final say, sure the devil can tempt us but God has the say of what happens to His true followers and God sent His son so we can be healed, forgiven and given eternal salvation, the devil cant take that away. "It is written, by His stripes we are healed."

If we take a step back its really easy to see what is from God and what isn't from God. God tells us that if we follow Him we will bear His fruit, we will live in peace, joy and happiness. He doesn't tell us that if we follow Him we will deal with depression and mental illness and sadness. **1 John 4:17** says, *"Love has been perfected among us in this: that we may have boldness in the day of judgment; because as He is, so are we in this world."* Meditate on that, as He is so are we in this world. As Christ is, so are we in this world. Jesus is seated at the Father's right hand, and so are we. **Psalm 110:1-2** says, *" Sit at My right hand, till I make Your enemies Your footstool,"* anything that comes against you and Gods word is your enemy and God has put it beneath you because as He is, so are we of this world.

Is it possible to be as He is, while dealing with sickness? No. Is it possible to be stressed or anxious while having a sound mind(**2 Timothy 1:7**)? No. Is it possible to follow Gods will but lose hope and a prosperous future? No, because **Jeremiah 29:11** tells us that the Lord has plans to prosper us and not to harm us, plans to give us hope and a future. Read Gods word, find what he promises us and anything that comes against it, cast it out and declare It Is Written. The thief comes to steal, kill and destroy, but Jesus has come so that you might have life, life in all its fullness. He says fullness, not emptiness. Be educated on Gods word and you will be able to tell what is a spiritual attack trying to bring harm because it will always go against the word of God. **Psalm 91:16** says, *"With long life I will satisfy him, and show him My salvation."* This tells us its Gods will for us to live a long life and know Gods salvation, anything threatening this needs to go, just declare aloud, "It is written, with long life He will satisfy me, in Jesus name."

I had a family member who was going through a rough time, his college plans were taken away and he was left to change his path, but he didn't know how, he didn't know Jesus and he was lost. He turned to his family but his family was lost as well dealing with a death, they were consumed in alcohol and weren't able to help themselves let alone him, so they sent him to a doctor and the doctor gave him a bunch of psychiatric medications and called it a day. Only things got worse. The spirit of depression sank in hard and then all of the medication made him worse because it numbed him from the pain rather then allowing him to work through the pain and move forward, he became zombie like. The spirit of addiction sank into his family after the spirit of trauma opened the door after their love one passed who was also, ironically taken from the spirit of addiction on someone else, he was hit by a drunk driver. None of these people knew Jesus and were all opened targets.

The spirit of adultery got to his girlfriend and she cheated on him, causing him to be attacked by the spirit of jealousy that Numbers chapter 5 talks about and it made his depression get a bigger grip on him. Once the spirits of depression, jealousy and addiction were there then came the spirits of anger, frustration and suicide. Shortly after he took his own life, and his family instantly felt guilt. They started blaming everyone they could think of and drank even more and nothing got better. This is how spirits work, they come in one at a time slowly, then they multiple and their goal is to take you from God and his plan for you anyway they can. We can look at problems one of two ways, we can see it spiritually like we are supposed to and realize Jesus already beat this at the cross and cast it out and declare Gods word over it. Or, you can accept the problem as the world does and deal with it in a fleshly, worldly way.

Galatians tells us the desires of the flesh are against the spirit, and the desires of the spirit are against the flesh, for these are opposed to each other to keep you from doing things that are bad for you. Our flesh is in its natural state to sin, we have to fight against that by being of the spirit. Our sinful flesh can crave getting drunk, adultery, pornography, fits of rage, jealousy and more.

It starts in the spiritual realm first, and when the attack makes it to your flesh you can either act on it, or see it as a spiritual attack on our flesh and cast it out and demand It Is Written and give the bible verse that supports it, but believe it as you say it. It is done as we believe, when you cast something out believe it, visually picture your spirit man kicking the butt of an evil spirit, forcing it to leave far away from you because Jesus is within you and as He is so are you, and because of that you have the authority to rid these spiritual attacks on your spirit and your flesh. **Luke 10:19** says, " *Behold, I give you the authority to trample on serpents and scorpions, and over all the power of the enemy, and nothing shall by any means hurt you."* He says nothing will hurt you, nothing.

Don't believe the lie the devil wants you to think and believe in worldly diseases or the worldly wants and desires, because you are not of this world, you cant be if you are as He is, and you are. Jesus makes it clear in **John 17:16**, *"They are not of the world, just as I am not of the world."* He is not of this world, and neither are we, as His followers. We are not of this world yet we arc in this word, He then prays to God to keep us safe from the doings of the evil one and to protect us while we are in this world. Though we are in this world we are not of this world, and worldly issues don't apply to us, we may be tempted and attacked by them, but we have the power through Jesus to rise above and take our seats at His right hand and thats what we need to do. Jesus asks for us to be sanctified in His truth, which his the word of God, this is the key, the answer to everything.

If we choose to live of the flesh and live by fleshly acts: sexual immorality, impurity, sensuality, idolatry, sorcery, enmity, strife, jealous, fits of anger, rivalries, dissentions, divisions, envy, drunkenness, orgies and things like these then we are not walking with God and we have become of this world. We must see these things as fleshly acts and follow the Holy Spirit who will guide us and show us the attacks and help us to rise above them. If you struggle with these acts and don't want to do them any longer, repent and ask God to help you, to replace your wants and desires with His and to renew your mind so that you wont want to commit these fleshly sins that keep you from walking with God.

Jesus teaches us in **Mathew 18:18**, *"Assuredly, I say to you, whatever you bind on earth will be bound in heaven, and whatever you loose on earth will be loosed in heaven."* Whatever we bind and loose here is then done in the spiritual realm, and then in the fleshly/worldly realm it is finished. If we cast out the spirit of addiction then it is done in the spirit realm so of the flesh we don't feel the need to use anymore, it might have to be done more than once, the devil is persistent, but we need to be as well. If we need patience and are struggling and we loose patience verbally, in the spiritual realm we are telling the Holy Spirit that we need help, we need the patience for our task and the Holy Spirit will provide.

2 Corinthians 10:3-6 says that, *"For though we walk in the flesh, we do not war according to the flesh. For the weapons of our warfare are not carnal but might in God for pulling down strongholds, casting down arguments and every high thing that exalts itself abasing the knowledge of God, bringing every thought into captivity to the obedience of Christ, and being ready to punish all disobedience when your obedience is fulfilled."* A stronghold can be visualized by a spirit literally holding onto you with a strong grip not to let go. The devil places strongholds on people to keep them insecure, sad, depressed, sick or fearful. But because we have Jesus, through Him we can break these strongholds and renew our minds and bodies. Satan likes to put controlling strongholds on women and carefree strongholds on men, why? Because when they marry and the women is controlling everything because she feels like if she stops nothing will get done because of the mans carefree attitude then things will be a mess, so she nags and is controlling and his carefree attitude becomes emasculated and annoyed. Its all spiritual, if the women were to cast out the stronghold of control and the husband cast out his stronghold of carefreeness then together they could accomplish whatever tasks they face without any anger or animosity. But too many christians forget they are not of this world and they assume these things are just normal and it tears families apart.

WHAT WILL YOU DO?

As I practice and focus on seeing with my spiritual eyes, I feel more at peace and I experience more joy. It is work and takes practice to train your mind to think and see differently then what the flesh wants you to do naturally. But with prayer and Gods help, we can choose to see things the way God wants us to see them. The battle starts in our mind, the devil will drop a thought or idea and he hopes that you will allow it to take root and then act on it, will you? Or will you see it for what it is and realize it is an attack for you to act of the flesh, and go against the spirit, to cause havoc?

Things are much easier if we take a step back and see it for what it is in the spirit. When my husband and I get into an argument I try to see it for what is happening spiritually, the devil trying to poke irritation at my husband so he gets mad and irritated with me, and then the devil poking confrontation on me so that I am prone to argue with my husband. When I realize what is going on spiritually, for me its much easier to take a step back and realize this is an attack and we are failing, but we wont lose. Because we then turn and give it to God and He will fix the issue for us so that we don't need to bicker. The devil doesn't like this, and he loves it when couples don't know how to see with their spiritual eyes, because they fall deeper into the fight and it can cause divorces.

The next time you are at odds with someone, will you

stop and try to see it with your spiritual eyes, or will you feed into the flesh and make the disagreement even worse?

I pray that after reading this, you can begin to decipher your past spiritually, to try to understand what happened and why with spiritual eyes so you can prevent it from happening in your future and you can prosper the way God wants you too.

CHALLENGE

The Rubber Band Challenge

Place a rubber band around your wrist and anytime you notice yourself say or thinking negatively, worrying, stressing, getting angry, sad, depressed, anxious, or contemplating moving forward with a sin, snap the band to make yourself aware of the attack that is being placed on you. To defend yourself and rise above the attack you must first realize and see the attack for what it is, if this seems too difficult just start by focusing on things that occur in your day that come against your sound mind that God has given you and the devil is trying to take away. Do this every day for a week, each day write down how many times you came under attack and what you did afterwards. Did you cast it it and declare the word of God over your situation? Find bible versus to stand on for these situations.

For example, as I was writing this book I started getting headaches whenever I would try to look at the computer screen which made it pretty hard to type anything or edit. I declared the word of God, "It is written, by His stripes we are healed. As He is, so are we of this world. Jesus didn't suffer from headaches so neither am I. Anything trying to come against this, spirit of pain, I bind you and your strongmen and I send you back to wherever it is you came from in Jesus name." I would then praise God, and I would see myself having to repeat this through the day, I would also take communion and pray in tongues throughout the day.

"Day 1" Example:

Day 1

How many times did you snap your band today? 15

What were you under attack by today?

The spirit of lies, spirit of nausea, spirit of fear, spirit of worry and heaviness. I was finding lies being told to me about my new pregnancy in my head, nausea, fear and worry try to overcome me with my new pregnancy.This was all mental and in my head, complete spiritual attacks from the devil trying to plant seeds of doubt in my head. He wanted them to take root so I would dwell on them and entertain it and believe his lies.

What Bible verses helped you?

Isaiah 53:5, *"But He was wounded for our transgressions, He was bruised for our iniquities; The chastisement for our peace was upon Him, and by His stripes we are healed."*

Day 1

How many times did you snap your band today?

What were you under attack by today?

_____

_____

_____

_____

_____

What bible versus helped you through this?

_____

_____

_____

_____

Day 2

How many times did you snap the band today?

What were you under attack by today?

_____

_____

_____

_____

_____

What bible verses helped you through these attacks?

_____

_____

_____

_____

_____

Day 3

How many times did you snap your band today?

What were you under attack by today?

_____

_____

_____

_____

_____

What bible verses helped?

_____

_____

_____

_____

_____

Before you continue with day 4, reflect on days 1-3. Did you snap your rubber bands less on day 3 than on day 1? The more time you spend doing this, the easier it will be to send the attacks away without entertaining them at all, thats what we want! The devil wants you to feed into his attacks, but we need to notice them instantly and not even entertain them at all, dont entertain the bad thoughts and lies he tries to whisper to you. As humans, we will always be under attack, but as Christians, we dont need to feed into them, we are called to rise above them.

Have you gotten in any fights or disagreements with anyone these last three days? Or judged anyone? If so, what was it about? How is the devil working in this situation to try to make you at odds? How can this situation be deflated, how can you see the person you may be at odds with without seeing the irritation or annoyance that the devil is trying to throw your way. Take a step back and stand in their shoes, try to understand why they see or think the way they do so you can have compassion for them and rise above the attack to find an aggreance.

For example, I found myself being judgmental the other day and I had to take a step back and ask myself why? My baby sister just had a baby and she is not only a new mom but very young and she also doesn't share my faith, so its safe to say we are raising our babies very differently. She had made a comment that she was already having her baby babysat so she could go out for some much needed adult time and I was shocked at how soon she was doing this. I had to stop myself in my mental argument and realize, she is incredibly young and if I were in her shoes I would probably be doing the same thing. Trying to see it in her shoes from her life and point of view I was able to better understand her parenting choices and realize that even though we both have babies, we really are at different phases in our lives and that alone will impact our parenting choices. Neither one of us is right or wrong, we just do things differently, but bottom line, its not my place to judge her, and I dont want to judge her.

But when I took a step back I was able to see that the devil was trying to get me to judge her and be irritated with her choices, but by trying to understand her better and thinking with compassion I was able to cancel out the judgment and understand her better as a new mother. We should never judge anyone, but when we feel under attack and feel like we are judging, stop, cast it out and try to understand their side with compassion and understanding, the judgment will leave. I am the only person my sister talks to who has a relationship with and knows Jesus Christ, if I sever that bridge by being wrongly judgmental, how do you think that will make her see God as? As Christians we are direct representations of God, non believers wrongfully judge God by our actions because thats what the devil wants from them. If I was mean and judgmental to my baby sister, would that push her closer to or farther away from God? Try to see it this way when you are at odds with someone. Or, you can do what the devil wants you to do and feed into the judgment, make a comment to the person that you cant take back and then end up in a huge fight and really hurting someone you care about, and push them further from God, What will you do?

Write down your last disagreement, fight, judgmental view or angry outburst. Could you have prevented this?

_____

_____

_____

_____

_____

_____

_____

Why do you think the devil wanted this to happen?

_____

_____

_____

_____

_____

_____

Did this act bring anyone closer to God?
How did you feel after it was over?

_____

_____

_____

_____

_____

Day 4

How many times did you snap the band today?

What were you under attack by?

_____

_____

_____

_____

_____

What bible verses helped?

_____

_____

_____

_____

_____

Day 5

How many times did you snap your band today?

What were you under attack by?

_____

_____

_____

_____

_____

What bible verses helped?

_____

_____

_____

_____

_____

Day 6

How many times did you snap your band?

What were you under attack by?

_____

_____

_____

_____

_____

What bible verses helped?

_____

_____

_____

_____

Day 7

How many times did you snap your band?

What were you under attack by?

_____

_____

_____

_____

_____

What bible verses helped?

_____

_____

_____

_____

_____

REFLECT

After doing this activity for a week, are you now able to better see the attacks? I have heard in the past it takes three weeks to break a habit or form a new habit. Keep doing this for two more weeks and this will help you to see things with your spiritual eyes. Don't diagnose issues with the flesh the way the world does, see it as the spiritual act that it is. If you are under stress dont give life to it by saying you suffer from anxiety, instead see it as the devil is literally attacking you with anxiety, cast it out, find a verse to stand on and say out loud, praise God, pray in tongues and focus on positive things and dont dwell on the negative.

The devil wants you to dwell on the negative so these fears will become your reality, dont give into it. See with your spiritual eyes so you can see the attacks and prevent them from taking root. It takes practice to be able to stop seeing of the flesh the way the world does and see with your spiritual eyes, but it is so worth it. Keep deciphering each day to become aware of the attacks so in your future, it will be come the natural for you to automatically see of the Spirit and see the attacks as they come so you can send them back to wherever it is they came from and you can keep living from victory to victory.

DECIPHER YOUR
PAST, SPIRITUALLY,
SO YOU CAN GROW
SPIRITUALLY FOR A
BETTER FUTURE

As I looked at my entire past and tried to break down everything Spiritually, my whole life made sense. I understand why bad things happened in my life to me and my family and why I was living with such worry and stress and fear. But when I broke every thing down and saw the spiritual attacks that led to our fleshly choices everything I was confused about became clear and led to God having me write this book. If I could learn to see spiritually by deciphering my past to make everything come together, so moving forward I can learn to no longer operate of the flesh and rise above the attacks by seeing with my spiritual eyes, then anyone can.

I challenge you to try, try to write down your testimony and decipher your life's story with spiritual eyes. You will be amazed at how everything makes sense now and the healing that you may need can take place. Trauma is a gateway to fear, if you haven't healed from a past trauma you have a door open to fear, and that isn't what we want.

When I deciphered my past spiritually I found out that I had unhealed trauma from having an absentee mother. I wasn't mad at her and I held no anger towards her, I understood her spiritual battle and still love her, but I didn't know I had to heal from the trauma of not having a mom growing up. After I healed from that, it was easier to kick fears butt away.

When I continued to decipher my past I understood

why I had two miscarriages, it was all spiritual and when I saw that the devil comes to steel, kill and destroy and thats what he was doing to me because I wasn't protected yet by the word of God because I hadn't been saved, all of my trauma from that was able to leave and I was able to heal from it.

Its therapeutic to go through your past, see things in a spiritual sense, heal from the traumas and learn how to see spiritually for your future so these things dont continue to happen. Give it a try, write down your whole life, then go through and decipher each part of it from a spiritual point of view. I pray that you will have the revelation that I had when I deciphered my past with spiritual eyes. I pray that you will be able to begin the healing you may need and the strength and wisdom to continue on, seeing of the spirit, and not of the flesh.

YOUR TESTIMONY FROM SPIRITUAL EYES